Winning
Techniques
for Players
and Coaches

Play Better
BASEBALL
for Girls

Bob Cluck

Major League Coach and Scout
Founder, San Diego School of Baseball

Play Better BASEBALL for Girls

Winning Techniques for Players and Coaches

Bob Cluck

CONTEMPORARY BOOKS

Library of Congress Cataloging-in-Publication Data

Cluck, Bob
 Play better baseball for girls : winning techniques for players and coaches /
Bob Cluck.
  p. cm.
 Includes index.
 ISBN 0-8092-9773-6 (acid-free paper)
 1. Women baseball players—Training of. I. Title.

GV880.7.C58 2000
796.357′2′082—dc21   00-60314

To my girls—Teri, Amber, and Jennifer—and to every girl
who loves to play baseball.
See you in the major leages . . . someday.

Contemporary Books
A Division of The McGraw-Hill Companies

1 2 3 4 5 6 7 8 9 0 VL/VL 0 9 8 7 6 5 4 3 2 1

ISBN 0-8092-9773-6

This book was set in Adobe Caslon
Printed and bound by Vicks Lithograph

Cover design by Nick Panos
Cover and interior photographs by Teri Cluck (models: Amber Cluck, Madison Bettis,
Hayley Laslavic, and Siena Nieto)

McGraw-Hill books are available at special quantity discounts to use as premiums and
sales promotions, or for use in corporate training programs. For more information, please
write to the Director of Special Sales, Professional Publishing, McGraw-Hill, Two Penn
Plaza, New York, NY 10121-2298. Or contact your local bookstore.

This book is printed on acid-free paper.

Contents

Introduction

During my 30-plus years at the San Diego School of Baseball, scores of girls have attended our school. Some have been excellent players. But baseball loses many fine female athletes to other sports, some because of old-fashioned attitudes and some because of pure sexism. Sadly, many girls are discouraged from playing or at least made to feel unwelcome.

Little girls play T-ball at age five, six, and seven with little or no inherent problems. At the caps level of youth baseball, or about age eight or nine, girls begin to drop out, with many less playing by age 12. Female players rarely play beyond this level. Girls who continue to play baseball into their teenage years normally have not only fine athletic ability but also strong mental skills. They must have these mental skills to simply survive.

Someday a female will play in the major leagues, and it may be sooner than some people think. When it does happen, I plan to be there to congratulate her.

Don't let anyone put limitations on you and what you can accomplish—even though you're playing a game that many think is only for males at the higher levels. Practice hard, do your best, and you may surprise everyone—including yourself. If you ever need help, please write me at the San Diego School of Baseball, P.O. Box 900458, San Diego, California 92190; or E-mail me at sdsbb@aol.com.

Hitting

Selecting the Proper Bat

Since 1971 we have taught nearly 10,000 hitters of all ages at the San Diego School of Baseball. One of the most common questions that we are asked is: How do you select the right bat for a young hitter? To be honest, many male hitters and their fathers can get so caught up in the power thing. *A heavier bat does not give you more power.* One has only to look to Mark McGwire and other power hitters to understand that this is true. While using a relatively light bat, McGwire is not just a big power hitter but knows the strike zone, keeps his balance, and doesn't overswing. How about Tony Gwynn? He has used the smallest bat in the major leagues to win eight batting titles. Using a bat that is even a little bit too heavy will cause a variety of mechanical hitting problems.

- A heavy bat forces you to use your larger muscle groups (shoulders) to help get the bat started. This in turn causes you to pull away from the ball with your front side, which means you see the ball poorly and have trouble with pitches on the outside half of the plate.

- Using a heavy bat costs you bat speed, which means you will have to start the bat forward earlier in order to hit the pitch fair. Since you're starting the bat forward earlier, you will most likely be fooled with any off-speed pitch like a curve or change-up.

- Too big a bat can cause damage to your swing in the form of bad habits that are very difficult to correct.

You can't grow into a bat unless you are satisfied with hitting .150 while waiting for your body to catch up with your new, heavy, powerful model. *Good hitting is about controlling your mind, your body, and your bat.* A bat that is a little light for you is a wise choice for any hitter at any level. Learn to become a good, fundamental line-drive hitter first and the power will come with maturity. We have developed the following chart to help parents and coaches select the correct bat for most players.

Bat Selection Chart

Player's Age	Bat length (in inches)	Bat weight (in ounces)
6 years	25–26	16–17
7 years	26–27	17–18
8 years	27–28	19–21
9 years	28–29	20–22
10 years	29–30	22–23
11 years	30–31	23–24
12 years	31–32	24–25

Player's Age	Bat length (in inches)	Bat weight (in ounces)
13 years	32–33	25–26
14 years	32–33	25–26
15 years	32–33	26–27
16 years	32–33	27–28
17 and up	33–34	29–30

Bat weights will vary greatly with different styles and manufacturers. Balance is also a factor. The key is that the bat *feels* light to you. It is better to get a bat that's a couple ounces too light than a bat that's even one or two ounces too heavy. Obviously, a player's maturity is an issue, but remember that you can't grow into a bat.

Gripping the Bat Properly

Simply place the bat on the ground in front of you and close your hands around it. It is important that the bat is in the fingers and not in the fatty part of your hands (fig. 1-1). If the bat is back in your palm, it will cause a loss in bat control, and you will also get bone bruises more often (fig. 1-2). When you bring the bat up to your shoulder, it is *not* important to line

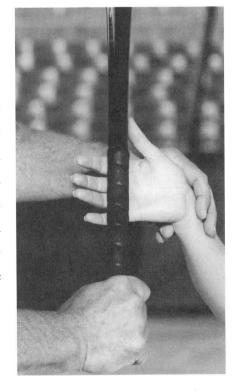

1-1 The bat should be held in your fingers to provide better control.

1-2 Never hold the bat in your palm. You will get bone bruises and a loss of bat control.

your knuckles up in any certain way. Everyone has different size hands and fingers. Your grip is *your* grip, don't copy anyone else's (figs. 1-3 and 1-4).

Your Batting Stance

By far the best batting stance for you is a slightly closed stance (fig. 1-5). Another very critical issue is where to stand in the batter's box. First of all, you must stand in the same place all the time. If you keep moving in the box, you will never learn the strike zone. I suggest you use this system:

If you are a right-handed hitter, place your right foot at the edge of home plate. Now place your left toe at the end of your right heel (fig. 1-6). Leave your left foot in that spot and assume your slightly

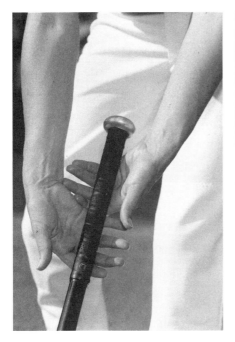

1-3 Place the bat down in front of you and then close your hands naturally.

1-4 Everyone has her own grip; your knuckles don't have to line up in any certain way.

1-5 A slightly closed stance provides for the best overall plate coverage.

1-6 By measuring one of your feet off the plate, you will be the correct distance from home plate in your stance.

1-7 This is very close to the correct distance from the plate for all hitters.

closed stance (fig. 1-7). This stance works well for hitters of all ages. Why? Because as your feet get bigger you will assume a position farther and farther away from the plate, and this system will self-adjust. From this position you can cover the outside half of the plate,

1-8 The head of the bat or the "sweet spot" should be over the heart of the plate.

and you can handle the ball on the inside corner as well. With a normal swing, your bat head (the sweet spot) is over the heart of the plate—right where you want it (fig. 1-8).

Tracking (Seeing) the Ball

As soon as you see the ball *in focus* at the release point, you begin gathering information about the pitch (its speed, trajectory, spin, etc.). This is called *tracking*. It is important to see the ball at the release point (fig. 1-9) and to get it in focus as soon as possible. In order to see the ball clearly when it arrives at the release point, you should first focus on the pitcher's cap. As you shift your eyes from the cap to the ball at release, it is instantly in focus. Like a camera, because you are already focused at this distance on an object (the cap), your eyes will focus on the ball quickly at the release point. If you simply stared out in space (at the point of release), you would have to first focus on the ball before you began gathering this critical information. The staring-into-space method costs

1-9 Keep your eye on the pitcher's release point to see the ball as early as possible.

you valuable time and is very inefficient. Hitters who use this method swing at bad pitches, freeze on the strikes, and are generally poor hitters.

Your eyes see the incoming pitch and send that information to the brain. Your onboard computer (your brain) determines what kind of pitch it is (fastball, curve, etc.), its location, and its speed, and sends messages to the muscles to react. The decision to swing or not is made when the ball is about halfway to the plate. The brain directs the muscles to move the bat forward at the precise time and to the precise area that the ball is headed in its flight. This entire process from release to contact takes about one-half second. It sounds impossible but that's what makes hitting such a challenge.

The Swing

While you are first gathering information about the pitch and deciding whether to swing or not, your hands trigger the bat—that is, move the bat back before coming forward (fig. 1-10). This movement serves two purposes: as a timing device to help you get the bat to the ball at the right time: and to overcome the dead weight (inertia) of the bat. In simple terms, it's easier to move the bat forward if you first put it in motion. There are lots of ways to trigger the hands. Some people bring their hands straight back; some bring them down and back up. Both are acceptable. Some coaches call going down and back up a "hitch"; but the truth is, as long as you get your hands back up before they begin their path forward, everything works fine.

1-10 When you stride forward, the bat starts back to "trigger" the swing.

Your Stride and Weight Transfer

While the hands are moving backward away from the ball, the stride is beginning toward the ball. Your stride should be soft and slow. You should feel as if you are picking your front foot up and putting it down in the same place. Consequently, a good stride will normally be less than six inches. The important issue involving the stride is that your direction is toward the incoming pitch and that you land at a 45-degree angle (fig. 1-11). If you land more open than this (fig. 1-12), you will have a tendency to fly open away from the ball and develop very poor hitting mechanics and balance.

Note: Your hands should arrive all the way back just as your stride foot comes down. The hands will then start forward to the ball. If your hands are drifting forward before your stride is down, you are drifting (carrying your hands) forward. You will have big problems with offspeed pitches and no power at all if you drift (fig. 1-13). I suggest using video to double-check this area.

1-11 Your lead foot should be at a 45-degree angle.

1-12 Opening the front toe is a very common problem that we see at the San Diego School of Baseball. This causes a variety of mechanical problems.

1-13 If you "drift" with your hands, you will lose all power and balance.

Balance and Weight Transfer

If you keep your head still, take an easy stride and don't try to over-power the ball, you should maintain good balance. If the emphasis is on your hands getting the bat to the ball with an inside-out swing, you should transfer your weight smoothly and completely. Your body weight should start out at 50 percent front and back, take the weight back to 70 percent back and 30 percent forward, and then back to 50-50 as you rotate, while your head remains still (figs. 1-14, 1-15, and 1-16). Don't worry about a follow-through. If you keep your head still, and hit the ball primarily to the opposite field or up the middle, you *will* follow through without thinking about it.

1-14 Your weight is evenly distributed over both feet as you wait for the pitch.

1-15 When you stride, your weight should go back slightly to your rear foot.

1-16 When the bat comes forward, the weight returns to 50–50 as you strike the ball. Your head should stay relatively still during the entire swing.

The Inside-Out Swing

As the hands bring the bat head forward to the ball, they must stay inside the ball and close to your body (fig. 1-17). If you extend your hands beyond the ball (fig. 1-18), you will cut across the flight of the ball. You will then have what is called a long (slow) swing and will only be able to pull the ball. By staying inside the ball you are developing what is referred to as an inside-out swing. This is the swing that is most effective for a hitter. Hitters with inside-out swings use the whole field, hit for better averages, and strike out less. It should make sense that a short quick swing would allow you to wait longer before committing to the pitch. Hitters with long swings swing at

1-17 Keeping your hands "inside" the ball is a real key to consistent hitting.

1-18 When you extend your hands early you develop what is called a "long swing."

bad pitches, can only hit the ball to their pull field, can't cover the outside half of the plate, and usually can't hit a curve or a change-up very well.

Drills to Develop an Inside-Out Swing

Using the Batting Tee. Place the tee on the outside half of the plate and then try to hit every ball to the opposite field or at least up the middle (fig. 1-19). Try to hit hard grounders and line drives and keep the ball out of the air. This drill helps develop a good swing as well as helping to prevent several other mechanical problems.

The Two-Tee Drill. Using two batting tees can help teach a hitter the concept of staying inside the ball. The hitter attacks the inside of the first ball and then tries to extend through the second ball. The hands stay close to the body as they pass the chest on their way to the ball (figs. 1-20 and 1-21).

1-19 Every hitter should use the tee regularly. Hitting off the tee properly will help solve many hitting problems.

1-20 and 1-21 The two-tee drill was developed by hitting instructor Reggie Waller in order to show the hitter how to "inside-out" the ball. To hit "through" the second ball, you must stay "inside" the ball throughout the swing.

Note: If a hitter is cutting across the ball trying to pull everything, she will hit the first ball and be unable to hit the second ball at all. You should try to hit the ball to the opposite field in this drill. If you are not in an enclosed batting cage, use Wiffle balls for safety in this drill, as the balls can fly anywhere.

The Soft-Toss Drill. Have someone feed the ball underhand to you and try to hit the ball to the opposite field. Have the feeder move the ball around to different areas and heights in order to make you adjust. Don't try to be powerful or try to pull the ball.

Pull Hitters

My favorite saying is that there is nothing wrong with pulling the ball, but a lot wrong with *trying* to pull the ball. Hitters who try to pull everything limit themselves greatly. Everyone should try to hit the ball to all fields. A hitter should think that every pitch is going to be on the outside half and prepare that way. You must have confidence that you can react and get to (pull) the ball if it is inside.

Bunting

Sacrifice Bunting

I prefer the square-around method of bunting (fig. 1-22). Another method of sacrifice bunting uses the pivot (fig. 1-23). Regardless of the method you use, you should place the bat at the top of your strike zone at the desired angle (depending on where you want to bunt the ball) and work down from there. Use your legs to bend and get to pitches lower than your hands. Pitches above your hands are balls, so

1-22 The square-around bunting position provides for the best plate coverage and is the all-around most efficient. Remember to set the angle early (wherever you want the ball to go).

1-23 Most players today use the pivot method of bunting, even though a hitter can't reach a pitch low and away in the strike zone.

you should pull the bat back and take those. You kill the ball (take the speed out of the bunt) by taking both hands back equally so as not to change the angle of the bat. If there is a runner on first base only, you should bunt the ball toward the first base line about four or five feet off the line. When there are runners on first and second, you should bunt the ball toward the third baseman and somewhat harder in order to get it past the pitcher, whose job it is to cover the line.

Bunting for a Base Hit

You may choose to bunt toward third or first. Remember that if you bunt toward first, you must bunt the ball firmly to get it past the pitcher (try bunting directly toward the second baseman).

1-24 When bunting for a base hit, left-handed hitters should take one step toward the pitcher while bunting down the third-base line.

1-25 For a lefty to bunt the ball toward first for a hit, she should step directly toward the second baseman.

Left-handed hitters should take one step with their left foot toward the pitcher and keep the bat level as they bunt the ball (figs. 1-24 and 1-25). Right-handed hitters should step toward the pitcher with their right foot while again keeping the bat level (figs. 1-26 and 1-27). There are more complicated bunting methods, but these simple ideas work. Remember that you don't have to be a fast runner to use the base-hit bunt as a weapon. If the third baseman is playing back too far, give it a try.

Squeeze Bunt

When you are called on to squeeze, remember that you can't give it away early. Wait until the pitcher starts forward with the throwing arm, then square around or pivot. A good squeeze is a ball bunted anywhere fair.

1-26 A right-handed hitter takes a step forward with her right foot toward the pitcher when bunting the ball toward third. Be careful not to step on the plate; if you do, you'll be automatically out.

1-27 Take a step toward the pitcher when bunting to first, but simply change the angle of the bat.

2

Pitching

In order to become a good pitcher you must have certain qualities. A pitcher who knows how to win becomes a valuable asset to any coach. The skills that make a winning pitcher are well within the grasp of any young player, male or female. Many pitchers in the major leagues have below-average fastballs, and there are many ways to get hitters out. If a female wants to go a long way in baseball, pitching is a good position choice.

A winning pitcher:

- Takes care of her arm with good mechanics and good judgment regarding the number of pitches thrown in one outing and proper warm-up and conditioning techniques.

- Learns a compact, balanced delivery to both maximize her effectiveness and keep her arm healthy.

- Has an effective change-up and breaking ball that she can throw for a strike 70 percent of the time.

- Develops a fastball that has movement (sink) and good control.

- Learns to recognize the game situation and uses her pitches wisely.

- Fields her position well, holds runners close, and takes responsibility for her actions (a must for all athletes).

The Pitching Delivery

I divide the pitching delivery into three phases:

- Windup—everything that a pitcher does before she gets to her balance point

- Stride/arm swing—from the balance point to the loaded position

- Delivery—rotation and throwing

Phase 1

A pitcher should begin her windup with the weight equally distributed between her feet. She then takes a small step back with her free leg (left leg for right-handed pitchers). She then lifts her free leg up to the side (careful not to swing the leg and lose her balance), as she reaches the balance point (fig. 2-1). This movement is not powerful or overly active, it is instead a balanced, controlled movement.

Phase 2

After reaching the balance point, the stride begins as the hands separate and the arm makes a semicircle and reaches the optimum height

2-1 Every pitcher must reach her "balance point," whether pitching from the windup or the stretch. This completes the first phase of the delivery.

2-2 When the stride foot is down, she arrives at the "loaded" position with the pitching hand up, back, and ready to come forward.

in its cocked position (fig. 2-2). These two events (the stride and the arm swing to the top) must match in elapsed time (the stride gets planted as the hand reaches the top). When the stride is too fast, the most common pitching fault, "rushing" occurs. The length of the stride is not a big issue. As long as you take an easy step, the stride will be very workable.

Phase 3

This is when a pitcher gets powerful. In this phase she rotates her body, brings her hand forward to release the ball, and finishes the delivery with her head down and out over her front knee (fig. 2-3).

2-3 A good checkpoint for parents and coaches is to watch the pitcher from the side. If the pitcher has her nose at least out as far as her knee, her delivery should be safe.

2-4 If the pitcher strides too fast, the pitching hand doesn't have enough time to get to the top, and the elbow ends up lower than the shoulder, causing big problems in performance and possible arm injuries.

Rushing: The Number One Problem in Pitching

When a pitcher tries to do too much, tries to throw too hard, or puts too much power into phases one or two, she rushes. Rushing refers to letting your stride foot get down before your hand gets up and back to the optimum position. When this happens, the pitcher will bring her hand forward from a lower position than optimum, and the result will be a poor delivery. Your elbow will be under shoulder height (fig. 2-4). You will throw the ball uphill. You will throw high fastballs and change-ups, and hanging (flat) breaking pitches. The solution to the problem is simple, just slow down the stride leg and let the pitching hand catch up. Taking an easy step (stride) will almost always help when things are going bad, and the elbow will be at least shoulder height when the arm comes through (fig. 2-5).

Arm Troubles

Nothing is more likely than a bad shoulder if a pitcher throws without getting her head out over her front knee when she releases the ball (easy to see from the side or with video). Your arm needs a full arc in which to slow down. When your head is not out over your front knee, the arc to slow the arm is very short.

2-5 If the pitching hand is allowed to reach the optimum height, the arm comes through with the elbow at least shoulder height or above.

This puts tremendous strain on the muscles that surround the rotator cuff (the muscles that slow the arm down after the ball is gone) and can cause major injuries.

Types of Pitches

Pitchers should develop at least three pitches by the age of 12; we recommend a fastball, a curve, and a change-up.

The Fastball

There are two basic grips for a fastball: The four-seam fastball (fig. 2-6) is the best one to learn first—it gives you the best control and

2-6 A four-seam, or cross-seam, fastball grip provides for the straightest flight of the ball. This is the grip that should be taught to every player. If a player's hands are too small to control the ball (ages eight and under) she can place three fingers on top of the ball.

2-7 This two-seam, or sinker, grip is used by pitchers to produce spin and movement in their fastballs.

a straight flight. The two-seam fastball (fig. 2-7) sinks and runs; it's the one that I recommend most female pitchers use at age 12 and older. Every pitcher can't throw 90 miles an hour. Many successful pitchers have fastballs with below-average velocity, but they can put the ball where they want to. Having the ability to throw the fastball into different areas regularly will get the job done anywhere at any level. Pitchers must be able to locate their fastballs in, on the inside corner, down the middle, on the outside corner, and away, 70 percent of the time to be successful at the college or higher levels.

To control the ball this well, a pitcher must learn to use her head as a guide down these pitching lanes. Pitching lanes refer to the path that the head takes to the target. With very slight adjustments to the path of the head, an easy stride (which lets the process work smoothly), and lots of practice, you can control your fastball. Again, this is a must for a pitcher with a below average fastball.

The Change-Up

The next pitch that should be developed at age eight or nine (or as soon as possible) is a change-up. The grip is not nearly as important as people think. You need not copy a grip of some famous pitcher. Just open your hand, place the ball against the palm, and get comfortable (figs. 2-8 and 2-9) with the position of your fingers. When the ball is back in your palm, the maximum velocity of your change-up will be about 8 to 10 miles per hour slower than your fastball. This is plenty of speed change to fool the hitter. The concept is simple: Get your change-up grip and think fastball. Throw your change-up down the middle and try to throw it the same speed as your fastball (it will automatically be slower because of the grip).

2-8 and 2-9 The change-up grip: Place the ball against the palm, right where the fingers meet the hand. Close your fingers around the ball and get comfortable. This becomes your change-up grip. Don't copy the grip someone else uses.

Anything else that you do to slow the ball down will give it away to the hitter (she will see a slower arm motion).

Another alternative to the straight change-up is the split-fingered fastball (fig. 2-10), developed by Roger Craig and the San Diego School of Baseball in the late 1970s. If you throw this pitch with a very flexible wrist (like a fastball) and don't overuse it, it will not cause arm injuries. Pitchers with small hands can develop an effective

2-10 The "split" is dangerous if you split your fingers too far apart and stiffen your wrist.

"split" but should not expect to achieve the violent downward movement that pitchers with larger hands can get. Those people in baseball who don't know how to teach the splitter claim it destroys arms. It was originally meant to be a change-up and should never be shoved way back in the hand like some pitchers do.

The Curveball

When learning a curve for the first time (ages 11–12), you should try to make the ball break straight down. If the ball breaks from side to side, you are throwing it wrong, with elbow injury a good possibility. Let's not kid each other: pitchers at this age will start spinning the ball in order to compete. Coaches and parents should face that fact and teach pitchers the proper (and relatively safe) way to throw the curve: Place the middle finger across the large seam and place the thumb directly underneath the ball. Point the index finger at your target, reach out in front, and simply throw the ball. If you point the index finger at the target and don't try to twist the ball from side to side, the ball has to spin properly (figs. 2-11, 2-12, and 2-13). Again, if the ball is breaking nearly straight down and not side to side, you're doing it right. After you have become very good at throwing it, simply put the finger down.

Now, don't fall in love with it. Don't throw it more than 20 percent of the time and you won't hurt yourself. Remember that you (and everyone else) are primarily a fastball pitcher.

2-11, 2-12, and 2-13 Place the middle finger on a seam, place the thumb directly across from your middle finger. If you point the index finger at your target and just throw the ball, the ball will spin properly. These are three different angles of the same curveball grip.

Sliders, Cutters, Knuckleballs, and Screwballs

I just don't think young pitchers should concern themselves with these pitches. I do discuss them to some degree in my books *Play Better Baseball* and *How to Hit/How to Pitch*, but they should only be thrown by players out of high school under the guidance of a qualified pitching coach.

Using Your Pitches

A smart pitcher throws strike one and gets ahead of the hitter. Make the catcher sit down the middle until you get two strikes on the hitter. With the count of 0-2 or 1-2, you can take a shot at a corner, then get right back in the middle with a strike. The idea is to make the hitter hit the ball and not try for strikeouts. When you work fast and throw lots of strikes, the fielders will do a better job behind you and the chances of your winning increase.

Pickoff Moves

All pitchers have the responsibility to hold runners and field their position. It is your job to learn the balk rules when you reach the level that allows runners to lead off. The rules are the rules; however, they vary from league to league and sometimes from umpire to umpire. You should check with your league to find out what you can and can't do in regard to balks. When you attempt a pickoff move to first, you must step over a line formed with a 45-degree angle (fig. 2-14). The same rule applies to a left-handed pitcher (fig.

2-14 When a right-handed pitcher attempts a pickoff at first, she must step over an imaginary 45-degree-angle line between first base and home plate.

2-15 The 45-degree angle is in force for a left-handed pitcher.

2-15). The move to second is essentially the same for both left- and right-handers: simply step back with your rear foot and pivot to throw. A pickoff move to third is not a major concern for any pitcher.

Fielding Your Position

When a right-handed pitcher fields a ground ball, she shifts her feet (called a "crow hop"), plants her right foot, takes her head to the target, and throws the ball chest high. The rule is to follow your glove. This means that right-handers turn counterclockwise and left-handers turn clockwise to make throws in the infield. Always take your time and make a good chest-high throw.

It's important that pitchers back up bases while a play is in progress. Try to get as deep as possible behind the person that you are backing up.

Covering First Base

A pitcher has to cover first base on all balls hit to the right side (the first-base side) of the field. Sometimes the second baseman will field the ball and you can stop, but you must break on every ball as if you will have to cover first. You first head for a spot about six feet up the line (fig. 2-16). From that point, start up the line and give the first or second baseman a target with your hands (fig. 2-17). After you catch the ball, step on the inside half of the bag with your right foot (in order to avoid the runner). After you touch the bag, push off to the inside of the diamond and look around for another play.

2-16 The pitcher heads for a spot six to eight feet up the line and runs parallel to the baseline from that point on.

2-17 The first baseman tosses the ball to the pitcher, who touches the inside part of the bag with her right foot in order to avoid the runner.

Becoming a good fielding pitcher can win you a lot of games. You should always practice your fielding and throws to all of the bases at least once a week.

For other defensive assignments, see Chapter 8.

3

Catching

Who Becomes a Catcher?

When a girl becomes a catcher she assumes the ultimate responsibility on the baseball field. *Catching is by far the hardest position in baseball.* Not only are the physical skills difficult, but the leadership requirements will challenge the mental abilities of any player. A catcher is like a coach on the field. She must work with the coaches and the pitcher and keep an eye on everyone else on defense. The defense is just part of the puzzle, for she must also try and carry her weight as a hitter at the same time. Most players are not willing to pay the price to become a good catcher.

The Catching Equipment

Your equipment should be of good quality and fit properly. Breast pads are recommended for appropriate age groups.

Receiving the Ball

A good receiver must begin with a good stance. When you give signs to the pitcher you should crouch in a comfortable position with your glove hand on the left knee to block the view of the third-base coach. Close your right knee enough to also block the first-base coach's view while allowing the pitcher to see the signs clearly (fig. 3-1). Keep the signs simple. Use one finger to signal a fastball, two for a curve, and three for a change-up. Hopefully, the middle infielders will watch the signs and it will help them get a better jump on the ball. Try to set up in the middle of the plate until two strikes. This will help your pitcher get ahead in the count. With a count of 0-2 or 1-2, you can move to a corner for a pitch, but then move back to the middle and get a strike. Good pitchers and catchers make the hitters hit the ball and keep walks to a minimum.

3-1 When a catcher gives signs to a pitcher, she should block the third-base coach's view with her glove.

After the sign is given the catcher should jump into the receiving position (fig. 3-2). In this stance, she is ready to move in any direction to receive the pitch in any location and to block balls thrown in the dirt. The feet are spread just slightly more than shoulder width for good balance. The glove hand is extended 75 percent, with the bare hand behind the back to protect it from foul tips. The head is up and the back is straight. Notice that the thighs are paral-

3-2 In the receiving position she should have her bare hand behind her and give a good target.

lel to the ground. The catcher should try to receive the ball with "soft" hands, bringing her glove toward the body instead of stabbing at the ball. This approach will minimize the number of dropped balls and help frame the pitches (help the umpire call strikes on borderline pitches).

Blocking Balls in the Dirt

You must block all pitches that are within your arm span. On pitches straight ahead, you should drop down to your knees with the glove covering the area between your legs and the bare hand behind the glove. The chin should be down to protect the neck, with the upper body angled so as to drive the ball down toward home plate to minimize roll after the block (fig. 3-3). You should not try to catch the ball—your job is to block it to keep any base runners from advancing. On balls to the third-base side, drive off your right leg to gain an angle to drive the ball back toward the middle of the infield (fig. 3-4). On the first-base side, drive off your left leg and create the same angle (fig. 3-5). Always remember to keep your equipment in front of you. If you turn your head, which is the natural instinct, you expose the side of your head to the ball. You won't get hurt blocking pitches if you follow the proper techniques.

3-3 The catcher must block the ball in the dirt whenever there are runners on base or two strikes on the hitter.

3-4 and 3-5 On the third-base side, drive off your right leg and create an angle so the ball is blocked back toward the middle. When the ball is on the first-base side, drive off your left leg and block the ball back toward home plate so the runner can't advance.

Throwing to the Bases

From your receiving position you must move early to the ball toward the direction of your throw. To throw to first base, step directly toward the target, rotate your upper body so that you are looking over your front shoulder at the target, and step toward first as you throw (fig. 3-6). To throw to second base, use the same method but be careful to go straight ahead to avoid the hitter (figs. 3-7 and 3-8). Remember that the catcher has the right to go toward second and

3-6 To throw to first, take a step toward first with your right foot, turn your upper body sideways and point your head toward your target, and step toward first with your left foot as you throw.

3-7 and 3-8 To throw to second, receive the ball in the center of your body and point your head toward your target (second base).

cross home plate with her momentum without interference from the batter. When throwing to third, take a step with your left foot, step behind with your right foot, turn sideways, and point your head to the target (figs. 3-9, 3-10, and 3-11). If the pitch is outside, step to the ball with your right foot (just like throwing to second) and throw to third in front of the hitter. On pitchouts the catcher jumps out into the opposite batter's box just as the pitcher is delivering the ball and follows the throwing techniques described previously.

Fielding Bunts and Pop-Ups

When a ball is bunted out in front of the plate, you should be very aggressive. Many times you are the only one who is able to make the play. Charge the ball, bend with both legs, scoop the ball with two

3-9, 3-10, and 3-11 To throw to third, take a step with the left foot behind the hitter, move the right foot behind you, then take a step toward third to throw. Remember that the hitter is moving forward to hit. If the pitch is outside, use the same method as throwing to second base.

3-12 and 3-13 On pop-ups the catcher should hold on to the mask until she finds the ball, get rid of it (away from the play), and then catch the ball with two hands over her head.

hands, and turn your upper body so that you are looking directly toward the target. Always turn clockwise so as to keep the play in front of you.

On pop-ups, pull off your mask (hold on to it), find the ball, get rid of the mask away from the ball, and catch the ball above your head with two hands (figs. 3-12 and 3-13).

Tagging Runners at the Plate

It is important that you learn to tag runners properly not only to get outs but to protect yourself. When a play develops at the plate, place

3-14 Your toe should point directly up the line at the oncoming runner in order to avoid serious knee injuries.

your left foot pointing directly up the line toward the runner (fig. 3-14). As the runner begins the slide, block the plate with the shin guard while tagging with two hands (fig. 3-15). Notice that the ball is in the hand and not the glove, making it impossible for the runner to knock the ball loose. If you block the plate completely (fig. 3-16) so that the runner has no choice, she will try to run over you. Nobody wins in this case. You should always give the runner some room to slide initially and then step in and block the plate.

3-15 Tag the runner with two hands, with the ball in your bare hand.

3-16 If you block the plate completely, the runner has no choice but to try to run over you. The catcher is usually the one who gets hurt.

Calling a Game

Young catchers should set up and give a target in the middle of the plate. Scouting reports are nice, but remember that when in doubt call the pitcher's best pitch. Most pitchers at the youth league levels try to become too tricky. Good catchers make the pitcher use their fastball and learn to have command of it. Remember that if you get ahead in the count, you are going to be very successful getting hitters out.

(4)

First Base

Receiving Throws

The first baseman must be a good athlete. Many times in professional baseball, teams hide a good offensive player at first and live with the below average defense. In youth league baseball that cannot be the case. You need a player at first who can catch the ball and defend poorly thrown balls from the infield. When you are covering the bag for a throw, you should set up with your heels against the bag while facing the person making the throw (fig. 4-1). When the throw comes, you should use the primary foot method to tag the bag. That is, right-handed people use their right foot (fig. 4-2) and left-handed people use their left foot to tag the bag (fig. 4-3). You should not stretch until you see the throw in the air. If you stretch too soon, you won't be able to reach tough throws (fig. 4-4). When a ball is in the dirt, start at the bottom (with the glove on the ground) and work up from there. By bringing the glove back to you (figs. 4-5 and 4-6), you will soften your hands and capture more wild throws, as opposed to trying to scoop the ball with a forward motion.

4-1 The first baseman should face the direction of the throw and not stretch until she sees the throw in flight.

4-2 and 4-3 A right-handed first baseman uses her right foot to touch the bag. This is called the "primary foot method." Left-handers use the left foot to touch first base.

4-4 If you stretch too soon, you can't react to a bad throw. You must wait until you see the ball in flight.

4-5 and 4-6 You should work from the ground up on throws in the dirt. Try to bring the ball back to you instead of reaching out and scooping toward the ball.

Positioning

The first baseman has lots of important responsibilities in regard to positioning and defensive game situations. If you are holding a runner on first, put your right foot next to the bag and give the pitcher a target. As the pitch is made, you move off the line two steps to prepare to catch a batted ball. If a grounder is hit to you with a chance for a double play, throw to the shortstop covering second (fig. 4-7). Try to make a throw chest high over the bag. Remember, you must retreat and cover first for the return throw (unless the pitcher gets there and calls you off).

4-7 Throw the ball to the shortstop covering second on the 3–6–3 double play. Notice that the shortstop and the first baseman are on the same side of the base.

4-8 The first baseman is the cutoff person to home when the ball is hit to right field and sometimes when the ball is hit to center (see Chapter 8). The stronger the outfielder's arm, the farther away from home she can set up.

When there is a runner on first and second or the bases are loaded, you should play behind the runner at first. Position yourself about 10 feet behind the runner. If you are the cutoff to home, you should have your hands up overhead and be in direct line with home plate (fig. 4-8). On bunt plays you must be prepared to charge hard and throw to the appropriate base. On pop-ups the first baseman has responsibility in many areas. See the defensive assignment chapter for these areas of responsibility.

5

Second Base, Shortstop, and Third Base

Choosing the Right Glove

Most middle infielders below the college level use a glove that is too big. Your glove should be very small and light in order for you to handle the ball effectively. The third baseman can use a slightly bigger glove.

Positioning

Aside from playing some hitters to pull and some to hit the other way, the infielders should understand the different depths they should play. Infielders in general should play deep in order to increase their range. This is back nearly two-thirds of the way from the infield grass to the outfield grass (fig. 5-1). At times infielders must play in to cut off a run at the plate. For this you should play near the cut of the infield grass (fig. 5-2) or just in front of the baseline, as your coach prefers. In most situations the infielders should play three or four big steps behind the baseline.

When a right-handed hitter is up, the second baseman has the responsibility to hold the runner at second close, and when a left-handed hitter is up it's just the opposite. Most third basemen play too shallow. There is no need to play in unless the hitter at the plate has shown you the ability to bunt for a hit. If you play deep and off the line, you can cover a lot of ground. If the ball is hit slowly, remember that you can charge the ball.

5-1 Most infielders play too shallow. Play deep and increase your range. Remember that you can and should charge the slowly hit balls.

5-2 When anticipating a play at the plate, an infielder should play directly in the baseline.

Pop-Ups, Bunt Plays, and Cutoffs and Relays

By reading the defensive assignment section, you will understand the immense responsibilities that the middle infielders have on pop-ups, bunt plays, and cutoffs and relays. One important thing to remember is that while going back for a pop-up, the outfielder has the priority and can call off the infielder. The infielder shouldn't call the ball unless she is under it and has stopped moving back. Remember not to call pop-ups too soon. Let them get to the top of their arc before making a decision.

Fielding Ground Balls

Infielders should start in the ready position before the pitch is made (fig. 5-3). When the ball approaches the hitting area just in front of home plate, the infielder should move into the fielding position with

5-3 This is the ready position for all infielders and outfielders as the ball crosses the hitting area.

a little preparatory movement. First move the left foot forward six inches followed by the right foot. This movement will put your body in motion and allow you to react to the batted ball more efficiently. As the ball approaches, bend with your knees and hips (fig. 5-4) and not your back (fig. 5-5). Make sure your glove is open fully (fig. 5-6). I know it sounds silly, but most infielders try to field the ball with a glove that is half open (fig. 5-7) because that is the way your hands hang naturally. You must turn your hand and work to get the glove fully open as you field a ground ball.

You must always remember to charge the ball whenever in doubt. Infielders who lay back and are not aggressive usually get caught in between hops.

When you field the ball backhand, keep your glove low and give with the ball to give yourself soft hands. When you field a ball going to your right, try to field it with your left foot down (fig. 5-8), plant

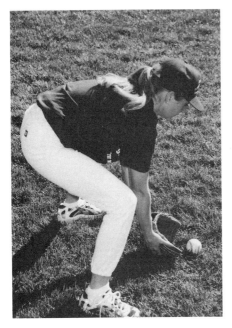 

5-4 When fielding grounders, players should bend with their legs.

5-5 This player is bending with her back, which is incorrect.

5-6 You must make the glove open fully when fielding ground balls.

5-7 This player has the glove half opened. This is the way your hands hang naturally and you must turn your glove hand in order to get the glove open.

5-8 On a backhand, try to get your left foot down when you field the ball.

5-9 and **5-10** On slowly hit balls, field the ball with your left foot down, and throw when your right foot hits the ground.

your right foot, and push off toward your target. When the ball is hit to your left, stay low, field the ball, close off your upper body, "crow hop" (get your feet underneath you), and take your head to the target.

On slowly hit balls, charge hard initially and then break down to short choppy steps. As you approach the ball, try to time it so you field the ball with your left foot down (fig. 5-9), switch the ball to your throwing hand, and make your throw as your right foot comes down (fig. 5-10).

Tagging Runners

When a tag is in order, you should straddle the bag, wait for the throw, and place the glove straight down in front of the bag with the back of your hand facing the runner (fig. 5-11). If you turn the ball toward the runner (fig. 5-12), she may kick it out or you could get hurt (spiked in the forearm with arteries exposed). If you reach for

5-11 On tags, straddle the bag and put the glove straight down in front of the bag.

5-12 It is very dangerous for you to tag with the ball facing the runner. The ball could be knocked loose, or you could be injured.

the ball, you would have to come back to tag. This is much slower. Don't leave the bag unless the throw is way off. If the throw is in the dirt, you must use your body to block the ball.

Double Plays

Good double plays begin with good positioning. Both the second baseman and the shortstop must assume a position closer to the bag when a double play is in order (runner on first with less than two out). From regular depth, take two giant steps in and two giant steps over toward second. This position is called double-play depth.

When playing shortstop and starting the double play, you will use one of three methods. If a batted ball takes you toward the bag, use an underhand toss to the second baseman (fig. 5-13). Of course, if

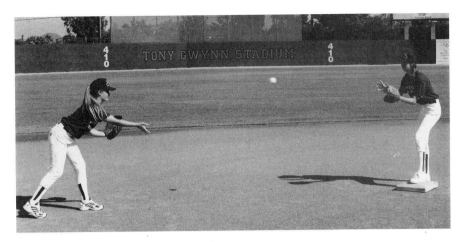

5-13 The shortstop begins some double plays with an underhand toss to the second baseman. Notice that the shortstop's momentum is going toward second base.

the ball is hit within a couple steps of the bag, you will field it yourself, tag second, and then throw to first. If the ball is hit at you or to your right, you will throw overhand to the second baseman.

When the second baseman starts the double play, five options are available. When the ball is hit within two steps of the bag, you should tag the bag yourself and throw to first. If the ball is hit right at you or just slightly to your left, you should make the backhand flip (fig. 5-14), pivot and make the snap throw (fig. 5-15), or toss it underhand

5-14 Advanced second basemen use the backhand flip to start the double play when a ball is hit right at them. This is very fast, but takes lots of practice.

5-16 When the ball is hit so that you must extend to catch it, rotate counterclockwise and throw overhand.

5-15 When using the snap throw, the second baseman pivots on the balls of her feet and uses a quick short throw.

just as the shortstop does on most double plays. If the ball is hit more than two steps to your left (fig. 5-16), you will spin counterclockwise, plant your right foot, and use the backdoor throw.

As the middle person on the double play, the second baseman should go to the base, delaying just behind the base until you see the ball in flight from the third baseman or shortstop. You then place your left foot on the base and come across the bag (fig. 5-17). As you receive the throw with two hands (fig. 5-18), you plant your right foot and step toward first base with your left foot. It is important that you step directly toward first with the toe of your left foot (fig. 5-19). If you step sideways with your foot, your knee can be severely damaged if the runner makes contact with it (fig. 5-20). If the throw is coming from the pitcher or catcher, the second baseman makes a semicircle and comes in facing the person throwing the ball (fig. 5-21).

5-17 As the middle person on the double play, the second baseman goes to the bag and delays behind it until she sees the ball in flight. Note that she has her left foot on the bag.

5-18 Receive the ball with two hands as you come across the bag.

If you are the shortstop and are the middle person on a double play, you should go straight to the bag and place your right foot directly behind the bag and give the other infielder a good target (figs. 5-22 and 5-23). When you see the throw in flight, then come across the bag to meet the throw. You should then take your head to the target (first base) and relax your legs. This is in case the runner makes contact with you. It is also important as a shortstop for you to point the toe of your left foot directly at first base to avoid serious injury.

Rundowns

When a runner gets trapped in a rundown between bases, it is her job to stay in the rundown as long as possible. This will allow other runners the opportunity to move up a base.

5-19 After catching the ball, in one continuous motion come across the bag and step directly toward first.

5-20 If you step with the left toe closed and the runner hits you, your knee could be severely injured.

5-21 The middle infielder should come directly toward the mound when the ball is hit back to the pitcher in a double-play situation.

5-22 The shortstop places her right foot directly behind the bag when she is the middle person on the double play.

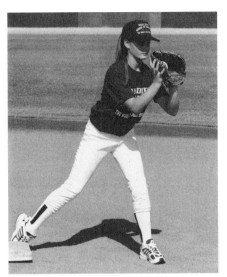

5-23 The shortstop should come across the bag and meet the throw. Her right toe will drag across the bag automatically.

5-24 The "charger" (the person with the ball) must run very hard at the runner, making her commit. The receiver (in this case the shortstop) gives a target, receives the ball, and makes the tag with one throw.

The job of the defense is to get the rundown over as quickly as possible. The person who starts with the ball (the charger) holds the ball in the throwing position and charges the runner very hard (fig. 5-24). The other defensive player, known as the receiver, gives the charger a target until the runner (now going full speed) gets within 20 feet or so. The receiver takes one big step forward and calls for the ball. The charger throws the ball chest high to the receiver and the tag is made. If done correctly, the rundown will be over quickly with only one throw made. Notice that the charger and the receiver are on the same side of the runner so no throws will cross the runner's path. It is advisable not to fake a throw, as you will also be faking out your teammate. Always follow your throw in case there are multiple throws in the rundown.

6

The Outfield

Selecting the Outfielders

When players begin playing youth league baseball, the outfielders are usually the last priority in team defense. The further you go up the baseball ladder, the more important outfielders become. Generally the rightfielder should have the best arm, the centerfielder should be the best all-around and be very aggressive, and the leftfielder should be the best hitter. I know this sounds funny, but if there is a place to hide an outfielder, it's in left.

Positioning

Outfielders need to pay attention to where the ball is hit. The centerfielder is the captain, and she should make sure when she moves one way or the other that the other two outfielders move with her. Outfielders in youth baseball play way too deep and hug the lines too much. They should play shallow because most balls are hit in front of them. And they should play "straight away" virtually all the time: The centerfielder should be a step or two on either side of a direct line from the mound to second base; the other two outfielders should be halfway between the centerfielder and the foul line.

Catching Fly Balls

Most outfielders at all levels get into the bad habit of drifting on fly balls—arriving just in time to catch the ball. You should instead get the ball as soon as possible, set up behind the ball, and come forward to meet it. You will then be in position to make a strong throw or adjust to a ball you misjudged or that got caught in the wind.

Learning to Go Back on Fly Balls

This is one of the toughest skills in baseball. Most coaches think that making the outfielders play deep is easier than teaching them to go back on the ball.

In order to go back properly, the player should take a drop step, and stay sideways to the ball (fig. 6-1). A simple drill can teach this skill effectively. Coaches can place their outfielders in a group in the middle of the outfield. Make them drop step properly, and as they are going back, throw them a pass (that's right, just like a football pass). Outfielders should never backpedal to the ball (fig. 6-2). As you approach the wall, stay sideways in case you have to jump for the ball (figs. 6-3 and 6-4). The outfielder next to you should help you by telling you how far you are from the wall.

6-1 The outfielder goes back properly by staying "sideways" to the ball.

6-2 Outfielders who backpedal will lose their speed, not see the ball clearly, and be more likely to fall.

6-3 and 6-4 Stay sideways as you approach the wall. Your fellow outfielders should let you know how much room you have.

Fielding Grounders

When no throw is in order, the outfielder should bend with her legs (fig. 6-5) and not her back—just like an infielder (fig. 6-6).

When a throw is to be made, the outfielder should charge the ball hard and field it to the side of her body. A right-handed outfielder should field the ball with her left foot down (fig. 6-7), do a crow hop (a little hop step), and throw off her right foot (fig. 6-8). She should remember to keep her head (and momentum) going toward the target as long as possible.

Catching Balls in the Sun

Every player has to learn how to catch fly balls in the sun. Most players make the mistake of thinking that sunglasses will do the trick. You must use your glove to block the sun (fig. 6-9). Sometimes play-

6-5 Bend with your legs and stay in front of the ball if no throw is in order.

6-6 When you bend with your back, you get very stiff and can't adjust to bad hops.

6-7 When a throw is in order, the outfielder charges the ball hard, and if right-handed, fields it with her left foot down.

6-8 Throw off your right foot and try to keep your momentum going toward your target. Tip: Try to grab the ball across the seams for a truer flight.

6-9 Block the sun with your glove hand. Remember, the ball may go through the sun on the way up and again on the way down.

ing the ball with your body turned slightly to the side will also help. You must practice catching balls in the sun on a regular basis and not just wait for the play to come up in a game. Then it's too late. It's a hard skill to develop, but you can be very good at it if you practice. You can practice safely by yourself by throwing tennis balls up in the air and catching them while turned toward the sun.

Backing Up Bases

The outfielders must back up every play in the infield. At the end of the game, the outfielders should be very tired if they have done their jobs properly.

Calling the Ball

The team defense is built around teamwork. It is very important that the outfielders call the ball clearly, loudly, and three times. To make the plays, and more important, for safety's sake, all players must be aggressive in this area. The outfielders have priority over the infielders for pop-ups and fly balls. The centerfielder has priority over the corner outfielders on balls hit in the gap. (See Chapter 8 for more details on defensive assignments.)

Hitting the Cutoff Person

If the outfielder overthrows the cutoff person, there is a good chance that the trail runner will move up a base. It is important that the outfielders make a throw with a low trajectory so that the trail runner(s) will freeze. The worst case scenario is one in which the outfielder throws high over the cutoff person, toward home plate, with no chance to get the runner, and the batter-runner moves up to second. This one particular case will lose many baseball games for every team, every year, at every level of play.

SAN DIEGO
SCHOOL OF BASEBALL
30 YEARS
"THE WORLD'S BEST SINCE 1971"
SAN DIEGO
SCHOOL OF BASEBALL
"THE WORLD'S BEST SINCE 1971"

7

Baserunning and Sliding

When you get on base, first check the number of outs, the signs from your coach, and where other base runners are. It's important to notice where the outfielders are playing, the score, and what your run represents.

Running the Bases

There is no reason for any player not to run the ball out. A few major league players set poor examples by loafing down the line. Every coach has the right to demand that all of the players on the team run hard on every play.

Getting a Lead

When you reach base you must work for what most coaches call a safe, maximum lead. This is the place that you can get back from so you won't get picked off. It is usually about one and one-half times your height. Never take your eyes off the pitcher while taking your lead.

You must also take a secondary lead. This is the ground you gain while the pitch is on its way to the plate. When the pitcher delivers the ball, you should take two quick shuffle steps and land on your right foot when the ball crosses the hitting area (home plate). From that position you can either plant and go back or cross over and go if the batter makes contact with the ball.

Making a Turn

When making a turn on the base paths, head for a spot about four feet outside the baseline and approach the base at an angle, stepping on the inside corner of the bag with whichever foot comes up in stride. You should always make a good turn at first base, especially if the ball is hit to left field. If you make a good turn, and the outfielder bobbles the ball, you can hustle into second for an easy double.

For all runners, the turns at second and third are primarily the same. When you go from first to third, you really don't need a coach if you have noticed where the outfielders are playing and know the strength of each outfielder's arm. You are always your own best coach when the ball is hit in front of you.

Remember that your job as a base runner is to score runs. Be aggressive and daring, and you will become an asset to your club.

Learning to Slide

Players love to slide. Any player can learn to slide once they understand the fundamentals. You will need a partner or coach in the beginning. You learn to slide on the grass, not on the dirt. Take off your shoes and sit on the ground with your left leg bent underneath you in the proper sliding position (fig. 7-1). Have your partner or coach drag you across the grass to let you feel a simulated slide.

7-1 Using a straight-in bent leg slide is the best. You will rarely get hurt with this slide. Remember to slide at full speed and in plenty of time.

You must keep your hands up as you go into the slide. A player gets strawberries on her hip when she turns to the side and puts her hand down (fig. 7-2).

Follow these three simple rules and you will become a sliding expert in no time:

7-2 If you put your hands down it makes your hip bone hit the ground. This is where "strawberries" come from (abrasions from sliding).

1. Always go full speed into the slide, and don't slow down.

2. Keep your hands up as you go into the slide.

3. Practice your sliding fundamentals regularly on grass without shoes.

When sliding into second to break up the double play, just slide into the infielder's left foot as she plants to throw. This is not an illegal move as long as you can reach the bag. You are not trying to hurt anyone; you're just disrupting the double play, and that's your job.

Never slide headfirst into any base, especially home plate. It is not only slower, but you risk serious injury.

8

Defensive Assignments

The following defensive assignments are used by most major league teams. They are workable for every level of baseball.

There are four possible jobs on team defense. Every player should be in one of these positions on every play.

- Getting the ball in your area

- Covering a base

- Becoming a cutoff or relay person

- Backing up the play

There is no job called stand and watch.

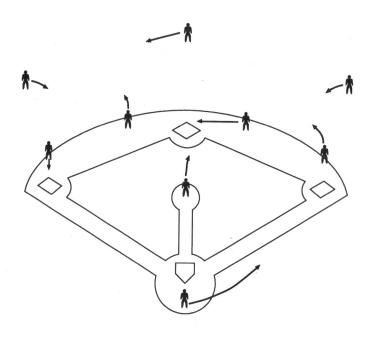

Single to left field—bases empty

Pitcher: Back up the throw to second base.

Catcher: Cover first base in case the runner makes a wide turn around first.

First baseman: Be sure that the runner touches first base and then back up the incoming throw to second base.

Second baseman: Cover second base.

Shortstop: Go for the ball; then try to line up between the leftfielder and second base and assume the cutoff position.

Third baseman: Cover third base.

Leftfielder: Field the ball and hit the cutoff person (shortstop). If she has been taken out of position attempting to field the ball, then throw the ball directly to second base.

Centerfielder: Back up the leftfielder.

Rightfielder: Move toward infield area in case of a bad throw from the leftfielder to second base.

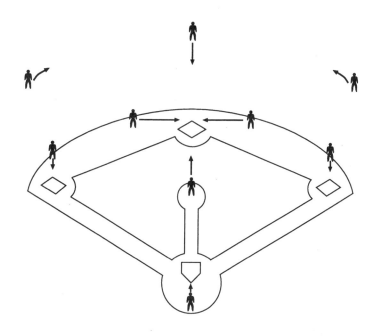

Single to center field—bases empty

Pitcher: Back up the throw to second base.

Catcher: Cover home plate.

First baseman: Be sure that the runner tags first base and then cover the base on the inside.

Second baseman: If the shortstop tries to field the ball, cover second; otherwise, back up the throw to second base.

Shortstop: Cover second base unless you go for the ball and are out of position and can't get back.

Third baseman: Cover third base.

Leftfielder: Back up the centerfielder.

Centerfielder: Field the ball and throw it to second base on one hop.

Rightfielder: Back up the centerfielder.

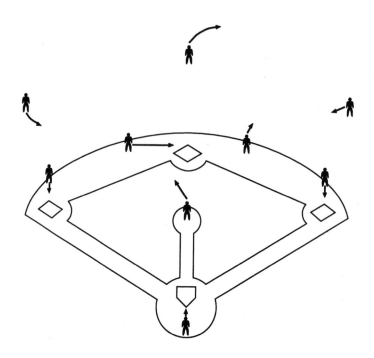

Single to right field—bases empty

Pitcher: Back up the throw to second base.

Catcher: Cover home plate.

First baseman: Be sure that the runner touches first base and then cover the base on the inside. (If you have tried to field the ball, you may be taken out of position.)

Second baseman: Go for the ball; then try to line up between the rightfielder and second base and assume the cutoff position.

Shortstop: Cover second base.

Third baseman: Cover third base.

Leftfielder: Move toward the infield area in case of a bad throw from the rightfielder to second base.

Centerfielder: Back up the rightfielder.

Rightfielder: Field the ball and hit the cutoff person (second baseman). If she has been taken out of position attempting to field the ball, then throw directly to second base.

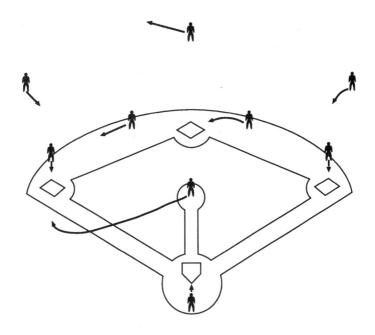

Single to left field—runners on first and third

Pitcher: Back up the throw to third base.

Catcher: Cover home plate.

First baseman: Be sure that the runner touches first base and then cover the base on the inside.

Second baseman: Cover second base.

Shortstop: Line up between the leftfielder and third base and assume the cutoff position.

Third baseman: Cover third base.

Leftfielder: Field the ball and hit the cutoff person (shortstop). If she has been taken out of position attempting to field the ball, then throw the ball directly to third base.

Centerfielder: Back up leftfielder.

Rightfielder: Move toward the infield and cover possible overthrows.

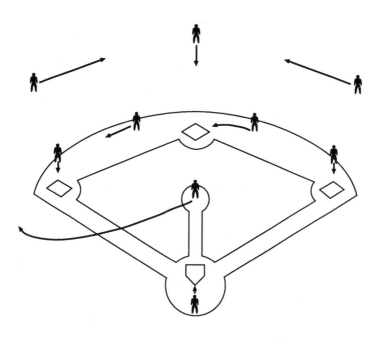

Single to center field—runner on first or runners on first and third

Pitcher: Back up the throw to third base.

Catcher: Cover home plate.

First baseman: Be sure that the runner touches first base and then cover the base on the inside.

Second baseman: Cover second base.

Shortstop: Line up between the centerfielder and third base and assume the cutoff position.

Third baseman: Cover third base.

Leftfielder: Back up the centerfielder.

Centerfielder: Field the ball and hit the cutoff person (shortstop). If she has been taken out of position attempting to field the ball, then throw the ball directly to third base.

Rightfielder: Back up the centerfielder.

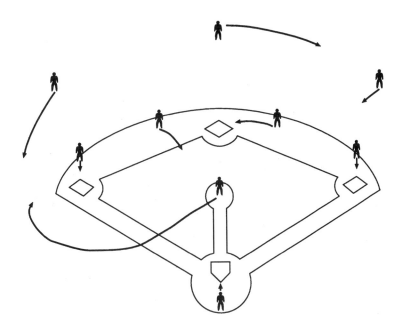

Single to right field—runner on first or runners on first and third

Pitcher: Back up the throw to third base.

Catcher: Cover home plate.

First baseman: Be sure that the runner touches first base and then cover the base on the inside.

Second baseman: Cover second base.

Shortstop: Line up between the rightfielder and third base and assume the cutoff position.

Third baseman: Cover third base.

Leftfielder: Back up the throw to third base.

Centerfielder: Back up the rightfielder.

Rightfielder: Field the ball and hit the cutoff person (shortstop).

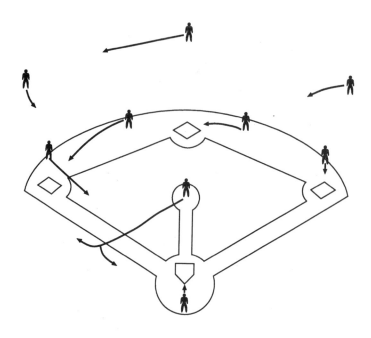

Single to left field—runner on second, runners on first and second, or bases loaded

Pitcher: Go to an area halfway between third base and home plate, read the play, and back up the throw.

Catcher: Cover home plate.

First baseman: Cover first base.

Second baseman: Cover second base.

Shortstop: Cover third base.

Third baseman: Become the cutoff person for the throw to the plate.

Leftfielder: Field the ball and hit the cutoff person (third baseman).

Centerfielder: Back up the leftfielder.

Rightfielder: Back up throws to the second-base area.

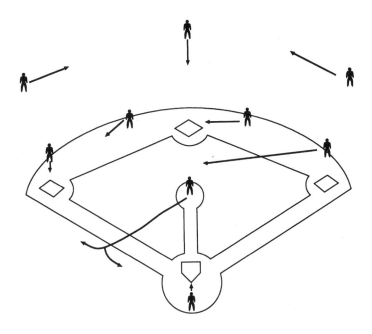

Single to center field—runner on second, runners on first and second, or bases loaded

Pitcher: Go to an area halfway between third base and home plate, read the play, and back up the throw.

Catcher: Cover home plate.

First baseman: Become cutoff person for the throw to the plate.

Second baseman: Cover second base.

Shortstop: Become cutoff person for the throw to third base.

Third baseman: Cover third base.

Leftfielder: Back up the centerfielder and help call the play.

Centerfielder: Field the ball, listen for teammates to call the play, and throw to either the first baseman (the cutoff person for a play at the plate) or the shortstop (the cutoff person for a play at third base).

Rightfielder: Back up the centerfielder and help call the play.

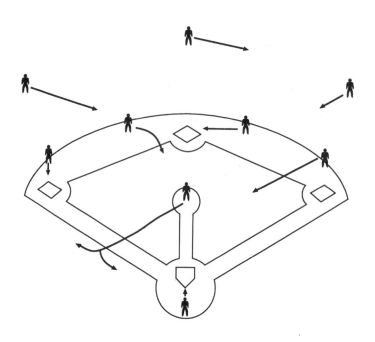

Single to right field—runner on second, runners on first and second, or bases loaded

Pitcher: Go to an area halfway between third base and home plate, read the play, and back up the throw.

Catcher: Cover home plate.

First baseman: Become cutoff person for the throw to the plate.

Second baseman: Cover second base.

Shortstop: Become cutoff person for the throw to third base.

Third baseman: Cover third base.

Leftfielder: Back up throws to the second-base area.

Centerfielder: Back up the rightfielder and help call the play.

Rightfielder: Field the ball, listen for teammates to call the play, and throw to either the first baseman (the cutoff person for a play at the plate) or the shortstop (the cutoff person for a play at third base).

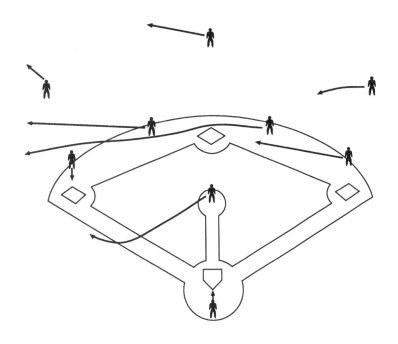

Double, possible triple, down the left-field line—bases empty

Pitcher: Back up third base.

Catcher: Cover home plate.

First baseman: Be sure that the runner touches first base and then trail her to second base.

Second baseman: When convinced that the hit is at least a double, assume a trail position 20 feet behind the shortstop.

Shortstop: Assume the cutoff position down the left-field line, in line with third base.

Third base: Cover third base.

Leftfielder: Field the ball and hit the cutoff person (shortstop).

Centerfielder: Back up the leftfielder.

Rightfielder: Back up throws to the second-base area.

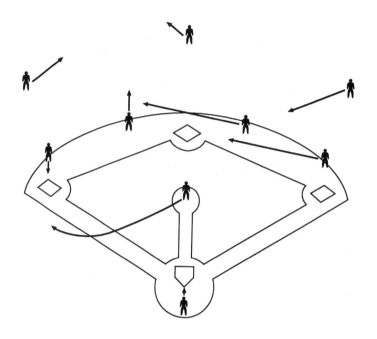

Double, possible triple, in the left-center-field gap—bases empty

Pitcher: Back up third base.

Catcher: Cover home plate.

First baseman: Be sure that the runner touches first base and then trail her to second base.

Second baseman: When convinced that the hit is at least a double, assume a trail position 20 feet behind the shortstop.

Shortstop: Assume the cutoff position, in line with third base.

Third baseman: Cover third base.

Leftfielder: Back up the centerfielder.

Centerfielder: Field the ball and hit the cutoff person (shortstop).

Rightfielder: Back up throws to the second-base area.

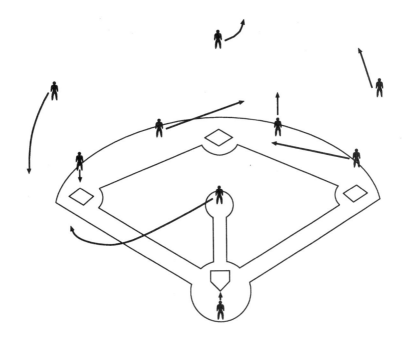

Double, possible triple, in the right-center-field gap—bases empty

Pitcher: Back up third base.

Catcher: Cover home plate.

First baseman: Be sure that the runner touches first base and then trail her to second base.

Second baseman: Assume the cutoff position, in line with third base.

Shortstop: When convinced that the hit is at least a double, assume a trail position 20 feet behind the second baseman.

Third baseman: Cover third base.

Leftfielder: Back up the third-base area.

Centerfielder: Field the ball and hit the cutoff person (second baseman).

Rightfielder: Back up the centerfielder.

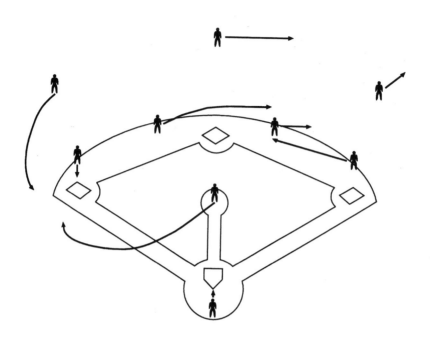

Double, possible triple, down the right-field line—bases empty

Pitcher: Back up third base.

Catcher: Cover home plate.

First baseman: Be sure that the runner touches first base and then trail her to second base.

Second baseman: Assume the cutoff position, in line with third base.

Shortstop: When convinced that the hit is at least a double, assume a trail position 20 feet behind the second baseman.

Third baseman: Cover third base.

Leftfielder: Back up the third-base area.

Centerfielder: Back up the rightfielder.

Rightfielder: Field the ball and hit the cutoff person (second baseman).

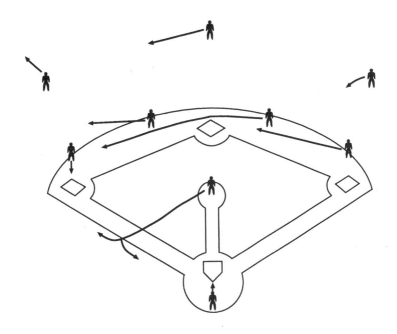

Double, possible triple, down the left-field line—runners on base

Pitcher: Go to a position halfway between home plate and third base, read the play, and back up the appropriate base.

Catcher: Cover home plate.

First baseman: Be sure that the runner touches first base and then trail her to second base.

Second baseman: When convinced that the hit is at least a double, assume a trail position 20 feet behind the shortstop. Tell the shortstop whether to throw to third or home.

Shortstop: Assume the cutoff position down the left-field line, in line with home plate.

Third baseman: Cover third base.

Leftfielder: Field the ball and hit the cutoff person (shortstop).

Centerfielder: Back up the leftfielder.

Rightfielder: Back up the second-base area.

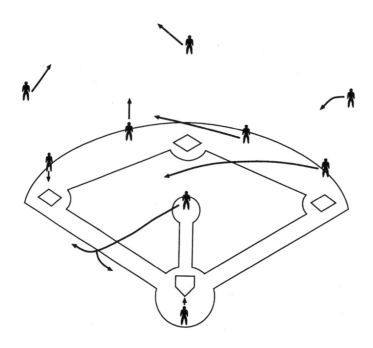

Double, possible triple, in the left-center-field gap—runners on base

Pitcher: Go to a position halfway between home plate and third base, read the play, and back up the appropriate base.

Catcher: Cover home plate.

First baseman: Become the cutoff person on the throw to the plate.

Second baseman: When convinced that the hit is at least a double, assume a trail position 20 feet behind the shortstop. Tell the shortstop whether to throw to third or home.

Shortstop: Assume the cutoff position, in line with home plate.

Third baseman: Cover third base.

Leftfielder: Back up the centerfielder.

Centerfielder: Field the ball and hit the cutoff person (shortstop).

Rightfielder: Back up the second-base area.

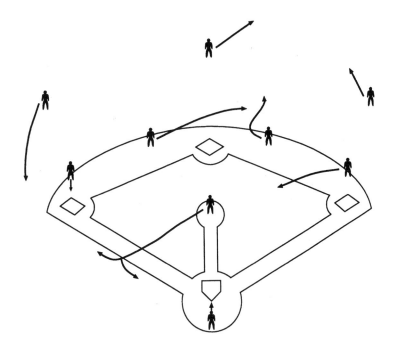

Double, possible triple, in the right-center-field gap—runners on base

Pitcher: Go to a position halfway between home plate and third base, read the play, and back up the appropriate base.

Catcher: Cover home plate.

First baseman: Become the cutoff person on the throw to the plate.

Second baseman: Assume the cutoff position, in line with home plate.

Shortstop: When convinced that the hit is at least a double, assume a trail position 20 feet behind the second baseman. Tell the second baseman whether to throw to third or home.

Third baseman: Cover third base.

Leftfielder: Back up the third-base area.

Centerfielder: Field the ball and hit the cutoff person (second baseman).

Rightfielder: Back up the centerfielder.

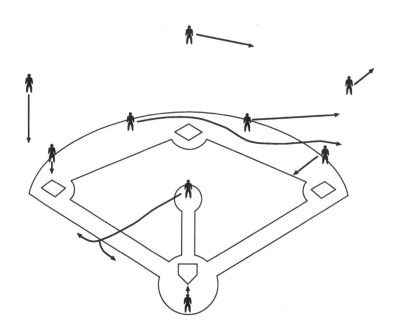

Double, possible triple, down the right-field line—runners on base

Pitcher: Go to a position halfway between home plate and third base, read the play, and back up the appropriate base.

Catcher: Cover home plate.

First baseman: Become the cutoff person on the throw to the plate.

Second baseman: Assume the cutoff position, in line with home plate.

Shortstop: When convinced that the hit is at least a double, assume a trail position 20 feet behind the second baseman. Tell the second baseman where to throw the ball.

Third baseman: Cover third base.

Leftfielder: Back up the third-base area.

Centerfielder: Back up the rightfielder.

Rightfielder: Field the ball and hit the cutoff person (second baseman).

Infield Pop Flies

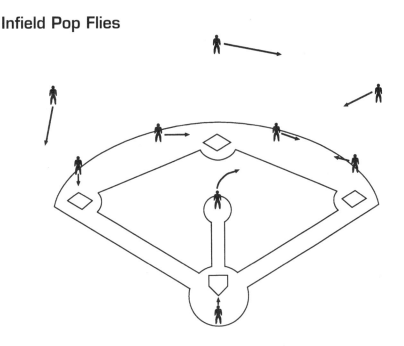

Pop fly to the right side of the infield—bases empty or runners on base

Pitcher: Help direct traffic and reinforce the "I've got it " call.

Catcher: Cover home plate.

First baseman: When the ball gets to the top of its flight, call loudly if you want to make the catch; give way if the second baseman calls the ball. Remember, the rightfielder has priority over the infielders on this play.

Second baseman: When the ball gets to the top of its flight, call loudly if you want to make the catch; give way if the rightfielder calls the ball.

Shortstop: Cover second base.

Third baseman: Cover third base.

Leftfielder: Back up the third-base area.

Centerfielder: Back up the rightfielder.

Rightfielder: When the ball gets to the top of its flight, call loudly if you want to make the catch. Remember, you have priority on this catch.

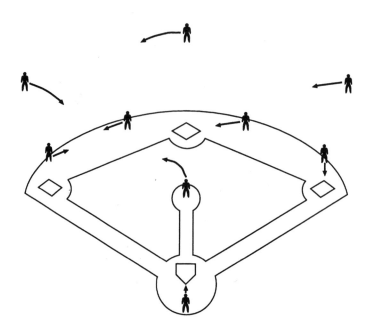

Pop fly to the left side of the infield—bases empty or runners on base

Pitcher: Help direct traffic and reinforce the "I've got it " call.

Catcher: Cover home plate.

First baseman: Cover first base.

Second baseman: Cover second base.

Shortstop: When the ball gets to the top of its flight, call loudly if you want to make the catch; give way if the rightfielder calls the ball.

Third baseman: When the ball gets to the top of its flight, call loudly if you want to make the catch; give way if the shortstop calls the ball. Remember, the leftfielder has priority over the infielders on this play.

Leftfielder: When the ball gets to the top of its flight, call loudly if you want to make the catch. Remember, you have priority on this catch.

Centerfielder: Back up the leftfielder.

Rightfielder: Back up the second-base area.

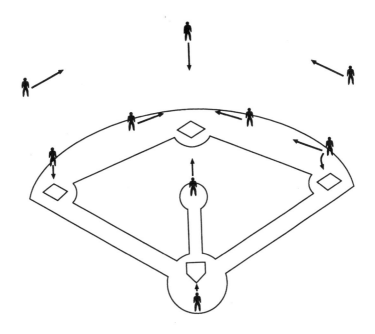

Pop fly to the middle of the infield—bases empty or runners on base

Pitcher: Reinforce the "I've got it" call. Cover second base if both middle infielders go for the ball and the first baseman doesn't cover.

Catcher: Cover home plate.

First baseman: Cover second base if both middle infielders go for the ball; otherwise, cover first.

Second baseman: When the ball gets to the top of its flight, call loudly if you want to make the catch; give way if the centerfielder calls the ball. If the shortstop calls the ball early, retreat and cover second.

Shortstop: When the ball gets to the top of its flight, call loudly if you want to make the catch; give way if the centerfielder calls the ball. If the second baseman calls the ball early, retreat and cover second.

Third baseman: Cover third base.

Leftfielder: Back up the centerfielder.

Centerfielder: When the ball gets to the top of its flight, call loudly if you want to make the catch. You have priority on this catch.

Rightfielder: Back up the centerfielder.

Bunt Defenses

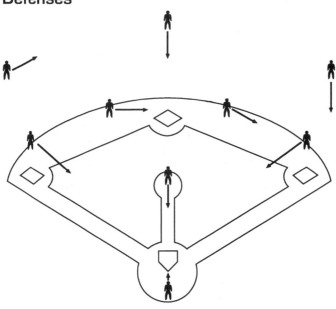

Sacrifice bunt—runner on first base

Pitcher: Throw a strike, cover the middle of the infield, field the ball if necessary, listen for the catcher to direct the throw, and throw to the correct base.

Catcher: Direct the infielders as to where to throw the ball.

First baseman: Hold the runner on first; then charge and cover the right side of the infield, field the ball if necessary, listen for the catcher to direct the throw, and throw to the correct base.

Second baseman: Cover first base.

Shortstop: Cover second base.

Third baseman: Begin on the edge of the grass; then charge and cover the left side of the infield, field the ball if necessary, listen for the catcher to direct the throw, and throw to the correct base.

Leftfielder: Back up the centerfielder.

Centerfielder: Back up the possible throw to second base.

Rightfielder: Back up the possible throw to first base.

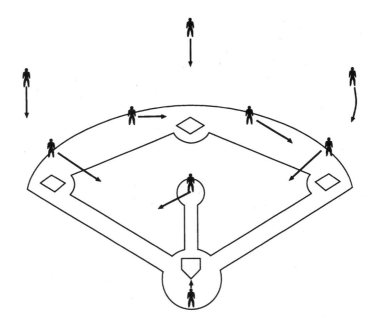

Sacrifice bunt—runners on first and second (standard coverage, designed to get the out at first)

Pitcher: Throw a strike, cover the third-base line, field the ball if necessary, listen for the catcher to direct the throw, and throw to the correct base.

Catcher: Direct the infielders as to where to throw the ball.

First baseman: Cover the right side of the infield, field the ball if necessary, listen for the catcher to direct the throw, and throw to the correct base.

Second baseman: Cover first base.

Shortstop: Cover second base.

Third baseman: Begin on the edge of the grass; then charge and cover the left side of the infield, field the ball if necessary (be aggressive and call the pitcher off the ball if necessary), listen for the catcher to direct the throw, and throw to the correct base.

Leftfielder: Back up the possible throw to third base.

Centerfielder: Back up the possible throw to second base.

Rightfielder: Back up the possible throw to first base.

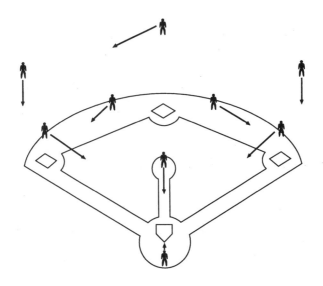

Sacrifice bunt—runners on first and second (the wheel play, designed to force the runner at third)

Pitcher: Wait for the shortstop to break for third. Throw a strike, cover the middle of the infield, field the ball if necessary, listen for the catcher to direct the throw, and throw to the correct base.

Catcher: Direct the infielders as to where to throw the ball (remember, nobody is covering second on this play).

First baseman: Cover the right side of the infield, field the ball if necessary, listen for the catcher to direct the throw, and throw to the correct base.

Second baseman: Cover first base.

Shortstop: Position yourself behind the runner, just off her right shoulder; break to cover third when the pitcher reaches the set position.

Third baseman: Begin on the edge of the grass; then charge hard and cover the left side of the infield, field the ball if necessary (call the pitcher off the ball if necessary), listen for the catcher to direct the throw, and throw to the correct base (a force at third).

Leftfielder: Back up the possible throw to third base.

Centerfielder: Back up the leftfielder.

Rightfielder: Back up the possible throw to first base.

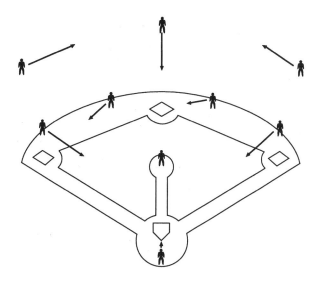

Sacrifice bunt in order—runners on first and second (pickoff play, designed to pick the runner off second)

Pitcher: Watch the shortstop break for third and throw to the second baseman for the pickoff.

Catcher: Cover home plate.

First baseman: Cover the right side of the infield, as in the wheel play.

Second baseman: Take a step toward first and then break to second for the pickoff.

Shortstop: Position yourself behind the runner, just off her right shoulder; break to cover third when the pitcher reaches the set position (although no pitch is thrown, you must break as if the wheel play were on).

Third baseman: Begin on the edge of the grass; then charge hard and cover the left side of the infield.

Leftfielder: Back up the centerfielder.

Centerfielder: Back up second base.

Rightfielder: Back up the centerfielder.

Remember that this pickoff play must be disguised as the wheel play in order to fool the runner at second.

9

History of Female Athletics

Little Girls Who Play Baseball

Girls who attempt to play baseball are usually nudged into their local softball program. Although I love Bobby Sox and other youth softball programs, I've always believed that more girls would play baseball if not for some hardheaded adults. Girls who do play baseball will usually have a wonderful and rewarding experience.

A young girl named Lindsey who has played baseball since she was 8 told me of her experiences when she was 12 years old and in her final year in Little League:

> In my first year, I remember during registration the people in charge insisted that I play softball. I didn't think I felt unwelcome, it's just that they kept telling me I was registering for softball. I just had to insist that I was playing baseball.

I've always felt kind of special playing baseball, and after I had a good year my first year, everyone knew me and accepted me. My parents always had to answer the question, why isn't she playing softball? Some other parents always brought up the fact that if I wanted scholarships I better start playing softball.

I remember that in my first year, the league's official program had a poem entitled, "Just a Little Boy." The last line read, "he's just a little boy and not a man yet." I don't know if it was just coincidence, but after I started to play, the league or the district removed the poem from the program the following year.

I have never been intimidated by the boys, because they just think of me as one of the guys. I have never been teased by the boys, maybe because I have hung in there with the best pitchers in the league and have gotten my share of hits. Other girls never tease me either. They think it's neat and they even come and watch me sometimes.

I have never felt that there are many differences in boys and girls playing baseball. Boys are more competitive in some cases and take the game too seriously. I would even see them cry sometimes when they struck out.

I wish other girls would play baseball. I think they would love it the way that I do. There is nothing to be afraid of.

Women in Professional Baseball

Before the movie *A League of Their Own*, most people never realized that women had ever played baseball professionally. Baseball Commissioner Kenesaw Mountain Landis banned women from participating in organized (professional) baseball in the 1930s. During

World War II the All-American Girls Baseball League (AAGBL) was formed and for several years was very successful. The league folded forever in 1954.

When allowed to play, women have become very good players. Toni Stone was a speedy second baseman for the Indianapolis Clowns, and two others, Connie Morgan and Mamie (Peanut) Johnson, also played with men in the Negro leagues. In 1931 a left-handed pitcher named Jackie Mitchell, while just 17 years old, reportedly struck out Babe Ruth in an exhibition game. Of course, after striking out, the Babe said he was just fooling around with the lady pitcher. To learn more about women in baseball I recommend the following books: *Women in Baseball*, by Gai Ingram Berlage, and *Women at Play*, by Barbara Gregorich.

Women in Other Sports

Women have been participating in sports for decades. One of the problems has been, and still is, discrimination. Some parents, and other people, because of certain attitudes in society, simply didn't think it was appropriate for pretty little girls to get sweaty and dirty playing sports. It was simply not considered ladylike to compete in most sports. Girls were discouraged to play team sports that were considered male sports. Girls who did try to play these sports were mistreated in many ways.

Broadcasts of the Olympics during the fifties portrayed the female Russian athletes unfairly as gross women who definitely weren't ladies. Some Americans may have been prejudiced by these images. Old ideas die slowly, but in the past 40 years women participating in individual sports like tennis and track and field have been slowly accepted by mainstream America. This has opened many doors for females in all sports.

In the late sixties world-class athletes like Billie Jean King couldn't even get college assistance. One of the first to receive a college scholarship was basketball star Ann Meyers, who attended UCLA. When King beat male tennis star Bobby Riggs on national television (Riggs was a 5–2 favorite), some people were shocked.

Even though women had run short distances in some international races, some uninformed people thought females would grow whiskers and would be unable to have children if they ran longer races like the marathon. During an early marathon in the sixties, Kathleen Switzer (who registered with initials K.V. to get in) was tackled by a race official because she dared to run. She had her race number ripped off her back and was never permitted to run again in the "for males only" race. In 1966, after her application to run in the Boston Marathon was turned down, Bobbi Gibbs ran anyway. After sneaking into the race and wearing nursing shoes (there were no running shoes made specifically for women then), she ran a respectable time of 3 hours, 21 minutes. But it wasn't until 1984 that women ran 26 miles (a marathon) in the Olympics.

Meaningful social change finally arrived in 1972 in the form of Title IX. Before this historical mandate, there was virtually no place for girls to play sports at the high school level in the United States, and women's sports accounted for only 1 percent of the athletic budgets at American universities. Title IX required schools to spend just as much (50 percent) on female sports as male sports. Although everyone doesn't agree on its implications, Title IX did give young women the opportunity to play, if they chose to participate in individual as well as team sports.

One of the real problems in the fifties and sixties was that women had no role models in most sports. Jackie Joyner-Kersee, Florence Griffith-Joyner, Lynette Woodard, Sheryl Swoopes, Mia Hamm, Dot Richardson, and others have changed that forever.

Do you want a great book about females becoming successful? Get *Cool Careers for Girls in Sports* by Ceel Pasternak, Linda Thornburg, and Deborah A. Yow. One of their stories is about broadcaster Robin Roberts, who learned her life lessons working for $5.50 an hour before joining ESPN and ABC television.

Try contacting the National Association for Girls and Women in Sports at 703-476-3450 or through E-mail at nagws@aahperd.org for some great information.

(10)

The Mental Game of Baseball

Confidence

Having confidence in yourself is nothing more than knowing that you have prepared well. In simple terms, if you are more prepared than your competition, you can play with confidence. Have you ever taken a test that you really didn't study for? Remember how nervous you were? If you've practiced hard and are prepared to play each and every day, you won't be as nervous before a game, and your performance on the baseball field won't suffer.

It is entirely normal to feel nervous before key events in your life. Baseball games, your first day of school each year, a big test, and your first date will all produce these feelings. The first thing to realize is that everyone is nervous when they play. I have been around many great major leaguers in my more than 30 years in professional baseball. I know people who are incredibly successful in business, music, and other endeavors, and they all have those feelings. Even the people who seem to be the coolest will admit that they are nervous when they play. You are not different or weird when you have those feelings.

When a player is nervous, that just means she cares. It is a sign of maturity when you can admit to having those feelings and deal with them the best way you know how. Nobody wants to fail and look bad, but competing against others is a very healthy thing. Kids who don't play sports miss a great opportunity to learn valuable skills that will help them the rest of their lives. These skills are important in business, in marriage, and in parenting.

Some girls get especially nervous at games because they have something special to prove. Female players have told me that they feel they are under a microscope on game day. Think about this. The pressure is on the boys to get you out. If you're the pitcher, the pressure is on the hitter to get a hit off you. This concept may help you relax and enjoy the game.

A System to Help You Relax

Nobody ever stops being nervous, but if you have a system in place to help you relax, you can control these feelings to some degree.

I've heard that some studies indicate that the heart rate of a player in the batter's box races out of control. The resultant increase in respiration can hurt your judgment and reaction time. Try taking two huge breaths just before you step into the batter's box. This will produce a calm feeling and bring your heart rate down. Many successful major leaguers, like Steve Finley and Mark McGwire, use this technique.

Another good idea is some positive self-talk. You may not listen to everything your parents or your coaches tell you, but you listen to what you tell yourself. Talk nice to yourself and you'll be surprised how this calms you.

Using Visualization

Players of every age and skill level use some form of visualization. You may already use these techniques. If you have ever dreamed about making a great play or hitting a grand slam, or even had nightmares about errors and strikeouts, you have used visualization both in a positive and negative way. The problem is, most players and some coaches and parents put too much emphasis on the negative things in baseball. The game of baseball is full of negative things. The best hitters make outs the majority of the time. Even the best teams in the majors lose nearly 40 percent of their games.

Try lying down in a quiet place before games (even lying in bed the night before) and mentally practice making good plays. Think about getting hits with the bases loaded or anything else positive. Throw out all the negatives. If a negative thought enters your mind, tell yourself *NO!* You should then think of something positive again. The more details in these mental pictures, the better. Add crowd noise or all the details you can to your mental pictures. Be nice to yourself and tell yourself good things. These practices make a huge difference in an athlete's performance. And you know what? It works in the rest of your life too.

Just before going up to bat, try taking the two deep cleansing breaths described earlier. Next, tell yourself goods things like, "I can hit this pitcher," or, "This is going to be the greatest day of my life," or, "I am going to hit the ball hard." Stay away from performance images like, "I'm going to hit a home run." Also avoid mechanical instructions like, "Keep my weight back," or, "Keep my head still."

Mechanics are for practice, and during an at bat you should focus on just seeing the ball clearly. As you will read later, coaches who shout tons of instructions at their players while they are trying to perform do more harm than good.

Practicing your visualization is a very necessary part of the equation. You should use mental images in your daily life on a regular basis to help you succeed. Before a test at school, see yourself getting your paper back with an A on it, or see yourself going up to the bulletin board and seeing an A next to your name. Positive mental images will help you perform better in every part of your life.

Learning to Deal with Slumps, Losing, and Other Failures

Failing is a natural and essential part of competing against others. Without failure, or at least mistakes, there can be no learning.

It is a must that you learn how to win and lose gracefully. Sometimes when a team wins even though they play a sloppy game, mistakes are often overlooked by the players and coaches. When this happens, the opportunity to learn from those mistakes is missed. Learning how to accept criticism from others is an important skill that everyone needs to learn. Recognizing your shortcomings, developing a plan to improve on them, and practicing to increase your skill level is a very important part of becoming a responsible adult.

Try to keep your emotions under control when things are going bad, and also when things are going very well. Don't get too high or too low. It's just the game of baseball, relax and enjoy it. It's supposed to be fun, you know.

Accepting Responsibility for Your Actions

Good ballplayers don't blame others for their mistakes. If you make an error, it's simple—you made a mistake and you'll try to do better next time. You are only wrong when you don't learn from your mistakes and/or blame others. Don't use excuses and blame other players, umpires, coaches, the field, the sun, etc. You are the one who made the mistake; learn from it, and move on.

In my opinion, most parents do a very bad job teaching their children to be accountable. Most kids are given too much, too easily, and too soon. When young people are not held accountable, they become spoiled, and this leads to an excuse-making irresponsible adult.

At games, parents and coaches who make excuses for losing, like, "The umpire really screwed us today," or, "Those guys were just lucky," are making a big mistake. This behavior is very destructive to the development of successful individuals.

What Are Goals?

Setting and working with goals are very important parts of your success in life. Goals are simply you expressing what you would like to happen in baseball and other parts of your life. Goals are the blueprints that you follow to success.

Stay away from baseball goals that you can't possibly reach. Goals should be fairly specific so you will know when you have reached them. You should have short-term goals and long-term goals. Be realistic and set goals in the short term that you can reach. Congratulate yourself when you reach a short-term goal and reestablish them regularly.

Coaches should discuss each player's goals and suggest ways that the players might attain them.

Why Set Goals?

It is absolutely necessary that you set goals for yourself. Without goals, you have no plan. Goals will give you a sense of direction as well as a way to measure how successful you are in life.

Some people don't set goals because they don't believe that they work. Some people don't set goals because they don't understand them. These people are probably using goals without even realizing it. If you have ever dreamed of the future, then in a way you are setting goals. Most people just don't realize what goal setting can do for their athletic careers and their lives in general.

Goals Should Be:

- Realistic. If you never reach a goal, you'll lose interest in the whole process.

- Short term and long term in nature. You must have incremental steps, called short-term goals, to reach your ultimate destination.

- Flexible. You may have to adjust your short-term goals along the way.

- Specific. Stay away from vague goals like "I want to have a good year."

- Written down. It is not enough to just say your goals; it is mandatory that you write them down, and even share them with someone close to you.

When you reach a goal, reward yourself with a small gift. Remember that each time you reach a goal you must set a new one. You will never run out of goals to set for yourself—*never*.

(11)

Proper Nutrition and Conditioning

Proper Nutrition

Ballplayers cannot perform up to their capabilities when they have improper diets. I can't tell you how many times I've seen young girls and boys rush into the ballpark for a game while gobbling a cheeseburger and fries, with a large Coke to wash it down. Young girls who participate in athletics need between 2,000 and 3,000 calories per day. Most athletes don't need any more than 10 to 15 percent fat in their diets. About 15 percent protein and 60 to 70 percent of calories from carbohydrates are recommended by most experts. These numbers should be adjusted for the age of the young lady and the sport in which she plays. With a sport like swimming or running distances, the calories should be increased as well as the percentage of carbohydrates. Healthy sources of carbohydrates are potatoes, rice, beans; whole grains are the best. Sugars should be avoided before and during athletic competition.

Athletes should eat between three and four hours before a game and have a normal meal. Nothing special is needed. A normal meal eaten four hours before competition will be digested before the game begins. When I was a kid, we were told to eat a huge steak or other protein before competition. Amazingly, over 40 years later, some athletes are told the same thing by uninformed parents and coaches.

Try eating several small well-balanced meals instead of two or three large ones during the season and you will feel better during the entire game. Don't fool yourself and eat poorly all week then suddenly change your diet to a proper one on game days. Your lack of a good nutritional routine will have very negative results on your overall performance.

Staying Hydrated

It is very important that athletes drink water before, during, and after games. None of the so-called athletic drinks are really necessary for the youngest players, as far as I'm concerned. Water is and has always been an adequate source for proper hydration for athletes. During strenuous athletic competition during a game or workout, your body can lose up to a half gallon of liquids, even more in hot weather. It is not enough to drink when you're thirsty. You must drink plenty of water before, during, and after you play.

Preventing Injuries and Conditioning Your Body to Compete

Ballplayers and other athletes who play hard are going to get hurt. A coach's job is to do anything and everything he or she can to prevent injuries. Regardless of the training methods implemented, injuries are going to occur. With proper conditioning those injuries will happen less frequently, they will be less severe, and recovery time will decrease.

Most adults don't have even the most basic training in treating injuries in their sons, daughters, and players. Some will say that people without this training should not be allowed to coach. The truth is, most leagues in most sports are desperate for coaches as well as other volunteers. The mentality of some is that bad coaching is better than no coaching at all, because without coaches there is no participation or program for the kids. All adults should be able to give basic CPR and at least recognize heat stroke and dangerous head and neck trauma as well as any other life-threatening illnesses or injuries. I would think every parent would want to educate himself or herself enough to potentially save the life of a child in an emergency situation on or off the field of play.

Conditioning Your Body

A proper conditioning program depends on the age of the player, the sport involved, and the climate in which you are playing. Baseball generally does not require a huge amount of conditioning, as far as endurance is concerned. Baseball is a sport of short bursts of speed and quickness of movement. Conditioning drills should involve performing baseball skills. In other words, you can best condition young players by having them field grounders, chase fly balls, and run bases. You can strengthen your body for baseball by doing sit-ups and pushups. You don't need weight training until age 14 or 15. Yes, females use weight training to enhance their performance at the high school level and beyond.

Developing a Stronger Arm

You get a stronger arm by throwing, not by lifting weights. Some adults like to say that females or males with poor arms "throw like a girl." Take it from me, and I'm an expert, just as many boys have poor arms as girls. It's a matter of technique and practice, nothing else. Gender should not be a factor. If you want a stronger arm, try throwing the ball more often and farther (after a proper warm-up). Try this simple program and watch how your arm improves (stay on this program for one month before your season begins):

Monday	Warm up; then toss the ball 120 feet 20 times.
Tuesday	Warm up; then play catch easy for 10 minutes at a distance of 50 feet, throwing to a target if possible.
Wednesday	Repeat Monday's program.
Thursday	Repeat Tuesday's program.
Friday	Take the day off (no throwing at all).
Saturday	Repeat Monday's program.
Sunday	Take the day off (no throwing at all).

As the month progresses, you should increase the distance slightly on Monday, Wednesday, and Saturday, depending on your age and arm strength. The distance you throw on these days should be close to your maximum when throwing the ball on a line. During the season, if you are a pitcher, adjust the program so that you don't throw long distances the day before, the day of, or the day after you pitch. If you are not a pitcher, this program can act as your warm-up on game day.

If you use this program, I personally guarantee you a better arm in 30 days.

Take Care of Your Arm

If you get any sharp pain when throwing anytime, STOP immediately and see a sports doctor. Some muscle soreness is normal, but sharp pain is a serious sign to stop. Remember, before you throw hard, you must warm up properly, which means playing catch for at least seven or eight minutes at ever-increasing distances until you approach your maximum. In my opinion, arm strength in young players has steadily decreased in the past 30 years. The reason is simple: batting cages and pitching machines. When I was growing up, if we wanted to hit, we had to throw batting practice to each other. There were no pitching machines to do the work for us. We threw more, so we had stronger arms in general. There were no video games and no malls to hang out in, so we just played baseball. The more you play, the more you improve.

Throwing is a very trainable skill for strength and accuracy. You can throw lightly every day and not hurt yourself. Remember to always warm up gradually before you throw hard.

12

For Coaches Only

Why Women Don't Coach

I really don't know why more women don't coach. Every year I offer a free class called "Moms Learn Baseball" and another for coaches (male and female) in San Diego. I talk to women about getting more involved in coaching, and I always seem to get the same responses. I'm told that women don't coach because they feel unqualified or they don't want to deal with the parents. Even ladies who take the time to attend a class like this lack the desire to coach. Women are league presidents, player agents, and team moms. They work in the concession stands and even umpire. Why won't they coach?

First, let's address the qualifications issue. It requires absolutely no playing experience to become a good baseball coach. Women can learn all they need about baseball fundamentals from books (like this one) that offer a wealth of advice. I can certainly recommend my book *Play Better Baseball* (NTC/Contemporary) as a terrific source for youth league coaches. Moms have a good relationship with little boys and girls and are much more patient than men are. Females are more likely to let the kids play and have fun, and are also less likely to put winning ahead of the kids. These qualities sound like the making of a good baseball coach to me.

Coaching Girls

Coaching girls is the most rewarding and easiest thing about coaching. Most girls are usually very enthusiastic, less likely to try to act cool when given instruction, pay more attention to detail, and are more likely to practice hard in order to improve their skills. Girls don't have anything to prove. They are very happy being a part of the team, and will generally do anything necessary to help the team win. They are void of the pressures of impending manhood, like being tough, needing to win at all costs, etc. My experience is that girls play the game for all the right reasons. They like to compete, have fun, and learn baseball. Also, females are more likely to learn from their mistakes and accept constructive criticism from coaches. In short, your relationship with your female players will be a wonderful experience.

Making Friends with Your Players

You can't teach anyone who doesn't like you, male or female. Regardless of the level of players you coach, you must first make friends. It is critical that you let the players have fun. You must create a team atmosphere and chemistry that promotes fun. These things are critical for male and female players from T-ball to the majors. I was considered a good minor league manager and major league coach in part because the players liked me (with a couple of exceptions). I gave them the necessary discipline and made friends at the same time.

Meet with their parents, ask the players about school, and spend some one-on-one time with each player, even if it's two minutes in the outfield before, during, or after a practice or game. Let them know you care about them as people. I know it sounds easy, but sadly, some coaches don't take the time. One of the biggest mistakes coaches make is to only talk with their players to criticize them. You must notice when your players do something well, and let them know that you've noticed.

A lot of parents do a poor job of teaching their children some essential skills, and maybe you can help in the process. Hold your players accountable and make them accept winning and losing in a responsible way. Don't make excuses for them for errors and other mistakes. Players will take on your personality if you do, and you'll have a team full of excuse-makers.

Working with Different Kinds of Learners

Different people learn in different ways, and it's important to recognize how your players learn as individuals. Some kids are auditory learners, some visual, and some are what I call "physical learners," in that they must try the skill themselves to learn it.

Auditory learners hear information, form their own images of what you say, and store the information for later use. Visual learners must be shown a demonstration of what you're talking about. Either you show them yourself, show them a video or still picture of the skill, or have another player show them how it's done. Kids love to be demonstrators. Visual learners simply won't learn as fast unless they see the skill. Physical learners must try the skill in order to learn it. You may have to grab their arms or feet and place them in the proper position for them to get it right.

Teaching Players More Effectively

When you are faced with the task of teaching young people a skill, you must follow a few easy rules:

- When speaking to your team, arrange them so everyone can see you and hear you clearly. Set up the short lecture away from parents and traffic noise; face them away from other practices or games that might be going on near your field.

- Speak loudly and make eye contact with your players one at a time. Some coaches habitually talk to (with eye contact) only one or two star players and ignore the rest of the team without realizing it. Auditory learners may not look directly at you while you're talking, for they are forming their own mental pictures of what you are saying (important for their type of learning). Don't get upset if everyone is not looking you directly in the eye.

- When explaining a fundamental, focus on it with a phrase, such as, "How to block the sun when you catch a fly ball," and explain why it's important for them to learn it.

- Keep your explanation short and simple. It's important that you demonstrate the skill in slow motion while explaining each step in the process (important for visual learners). For most, it is helpful if you number each step.

- Have the entire group stand in place and go through the movements of the skill (important for physical learners). This will familiarize them with each movement and also allow you to see which ones don't understand the movements you have described.

- Ask questions at the end and let a player or two come up in front of the group to demonstrate the skill. It helps kids when one of their own shows them the correct way (maybe you can't or don't want to demonstrate some movements).

- It's very important that you immediately let all the players try the skill as soon as possible (while it's fresh in their minds).

Also at the beginning of the next practice, review the material with the group from the preceding practice. A few kids will forget everything from one practice to another.

Organizing Practices and Looking the Part

If you are going to coach, at least have a little pride in the way you dress. If you look like you have no clue and are unorganized, players will not take your practices seriously. If you have no enthusiasm, your players will have none either. Since most practices are during the week, I know it may be difficult, but try to show up early. Have things organized, have a plan for the day, and push your energy button when the kids arrive. I know that you may have gotten up early and worked a full day, but the kids are fresh and ready to play and have fun after a day at school.

Nothing is worse for team morale than having a long boring practice. Players won't want to come to practice if they stand around while you throw batting practice and you throw 2 strikes out of 10. Run a short, snappy practice of no more than 90 minutes.

Begin with a quick stretching program that warms the major muscle groups and then go. Kids don't need some long, drawn-out warm-up program. Place them in small groups and run stations in order to cover many different fundamentals at once. *Make it a point to teach at least one new skill every practice.* Even play a little game situation at the end. The players will be excited about coming to practice each and every week. Keep the energy level high by rotating the kids on time to each station (see below). Always end the practice with something fun and positive (I don't mean a trip to McDonald's).

A 90-Minute Practice the Players Will Love

The following is a nice blueprint of an interesting practice that you can run with 12 players and no help. Divide your team into three groups of four players; you may want to use cones the first two or three practices until they know where to stand.

Station 1: Hitting Grounders to the Infielders

Put four players at home plate with bats. Have them hit grounders to four other players at first base, second base, shortstop, and third base. For younger players, or if you don't like the way they hit the balls, have them throw the grounders.

Station 2: Infield Grounders

Four players assume the first base, second base, shortstop, and third base positions. They field the grounders and return the ball to the hitters. You should have them take five grounders and rotate to a different position (1b to 2b to ss to 3b). Make them jog between positions as they move.

Station 3: Fundamentals with the Boss

Hit fly balls to this group. Spread the players out so they don't crowd one another. You can also use this station to place the players in a line from the foul line out toward the fence and have them relay the ball up and down the line. You can even time or count one round up and down and make them handle the ball and throw accurately. You can practice sliding here, tagging, rundowns, catching balls in the sun, and other fundamentals.

The players rotate from station one to two to three and back to one every eight minutes or so. Every time they get to your station, change the fundamental. Use sliding, pop-ups, baserunning, fly balls, bunting, etc. Use your imagination. The players will work on hitting, fielding grounders, catching flies, sliding, throwing, and handling the ball all in a 48-minute practice.

Play a game situation the final 40 minutes, and they will have a ball and learn baseball. This can be run on one field, by yourself, with 12 players and minimal equipment. When you have an assistant coach or two, the possibilities are unlimited. Keep track of the fundamentals that you cover, and change them with each practice. And always remember there is more to practicing baseball than just taking a long batting practice.

Coaching and working with kids is not only a great contribution to society; it's fun. Female athletes in particular bring a special enthusiasm to the field of play. I have found teaching girls the game of baseball very rewarding and enjoyable. I'm sure most coaches of female athletes feel the same way.

Using Video

Using video to reinforce teaching concepts is very beneficial. Coaches should be careful not to be too critical during these video sessions. If you embarrass a player in front of teammates, you have a problem. Use what is called a "positive sandwich." Show them good things, slip in a little constructive criticism, then another positive. People love to watch themselves on television, and kids are no different.

Remember to have fun. That's why you took this job.

A Final Note to Players

Since organized youth sports began nearly 50 years ago, a handful of adults in almost every league are guilty of poor behavior. When these isolated cases occur, they gain much attention and are normally blown out of proportion. Most coaches, parents, and other adults do a wonderful job, and most leagues now have strict rules about aberrant behavior during games and practices. Remember that there would be no fields and baseball leagues if not for the adults that hustle up sponsors to buy uniforms and work in the concession stands, as well as on the fields themselves. Where would youth baseball be without the volunteer umpires and coaches, team moms, and others who put leagues together? Usually the few adults who complain are the ones who just show up on game day, second-guess the coaches, and don't help the league to operate. The great majority of adults involved with youth baseball and other sports are there for all the right reasons.

Index

From widely respected baseball coach and author Bob Cluck, here is a book that will help girls improve their baseball skills at the youth-league level and beyond. This fully illustrated guidebook covers both baseball fundamentals and mental preparation for the girls of all ages who are joining organized baseball leagues in record numbers.

Play Better Baseball for Girls features core baseball instruction geared exclusively toward girls, along with more than 100 instructional photos. Also included is specific advice for female players and a special chapter for coaches who have female players on their teams.

Bob Cluck is a major league baseball coach and scout and the founder of the San Diego School of Baseball. He is the author of the bestselling *Play Better Baseball* and *How to Hit/How to Pitch*. Teri Cluck, Bob's wife, provided the useful photographs.

US $15.95 / CAN $23.95

ISBN 0-8092-9773-6

51595

9 780809 297733